About the Author

Edmund Jones was a minister for forty-four years in both the Church of Scotland and the Presbyterian Church, USA. He has taken a keen interest in the language of worship that is lively, evocative and appropriate. His services were frequently used on radio and television by the BBC and ITV religious broadcasting. Now retired, he is enjoying attending worship in Glasgow.

Prayers from Cathedral and Kirk

Edmund Jones

Prayers from Cathedral and Kirk

Olympia Publishers
London

www.olympiapublishers.com
OLYMPIA PAPERBACK EDITION

Copyright © Edmund Jones 2024

The right of Edmund Jones to be identified as author of
this work has been asserted in accordance with sections 77 and 78 of
the Copyright, Designs and Patents Act 1988.

All Rights Reserved

No reproduction, copy or transmission of this publication
may be made without written permission.
No paragraph of this publication may be reproduced,
copied or transmitted save with the written permission of the publisher,
or in accordance with the provisions
of the Copyright Act 1956 (as amended).

Any person who commits any unauthorised act in relation to
this publication may be liable to criminal
prosecution and civil claims for damage.

A CIP catalogue record for this title is
available from the British Library.

ISBN: 978-1-80439-696-4

This is a work of nonfiction. No names have been changed, no
characters invented, no events fabricated.

First Published in 2024

**Olympia Publishers
Tallis House
2 Tallis Street
London
EC4Y 0AB**

Printed in Great Britain

Dedication

I dedicate this book to my children – Jennifer, Jeremy and Jonathan – who often drove me to prayer but always with great thanksgiving. I also dedicate this book to my lively wife Dorene.

Advent 1

He will come and not tarry.

He will come when the trees stand naked and alone, when the winds are strong and the sun is weak, when sadness circles our lives and the night stalks our souls. He will come.

He will come when hatred mocks kindness, when the pitiless rule the earth and the poor are forgotten, when truth lies friendless at the gates. He will come.

He will come in the season of fatigue, the season of long nights and steep angry winds, the season when the ground is hard and darkness comes early and leaves late. He will come.

He will come when a star appears in the night, and an angel brings joy clothed in pain. When the old have their visions and the young dream their dreams. He will come.

He will come in the voice of a simple maid, the joy of a village lad and the welcome of a peasant home. He will come.

He will come when angels flood the hillside with song, and the people that sat in darkness see a great light, and the weary world learns to hope again. He will come.

So, come quickly, Lord Jesus. Come again, come now, and let our wounded world find its healing, our angry world find its peace and our broken world become family again through the cry of a child in the night, even Jesus our Lord.

Advent 2

It is the season of the cold, the dark, the dying – the time of sudden fears and the chilled silences of the wind. It is the season of things coming to an end. Watchman, what of the night? Cometh still the morning?

O ever faithful God who keeps his promises, open our eyes to the star in the East and our ears to the cry of a child. Open our hearts to a new beginning and the sound of angel voices far away.

Teach us to stand on tiptoe in the whispering sadness of a year coming to an end that we may welcome the accepted time and the day of salvation, that day when the forgotten will be welcomed and the starving poor will be present at the banquet, that day when heaven will touch earth and a peasant girl will be crowned with destiny.

Let joy come again to the world – joy to those who cry out for bread, joy to those whose families are in danger, joy to those who have lost loved ones over the past year, joy to those with anger in their hearts and bitterness in souls, joy to those who work for peace with justice and have no truck with dishonesty.

And let peace come to our lives too – peace for the imperfection of our discipleship and mercy for every wandering. Peace to free us from guilt and also from regret that we may live as your sons and daughters in a world that is being remade and redeemed.

So, let the kingdom come.

Advent 3

O Lord, if the deep darkness flees before the morning crispness, if the season of swift clouds, running winds and leaves spilled casts its strange contrasts around us, if snowflakes fall with heaven's gentleness in them, if fires blaze in the winter gloom and the evening lamps are lit, if laughter is still shared, generous feeling abounds and peace is born again, if each daybreak our hearts stand on tiptoe for the joys that are yet to come, if angels sing at midnight, old men have their visions and restless children dream their dreams, then are our souls made glad that the ancient promise is fulfilled; majesty has come to stable again on our poor earth, and the spring day on high has visited us.

We give thanks and bless the wonder of our days that light is come again. For the place we stand on is holy ground, not of incense or altar, but the cry of a maid and the coming of a child promised of old by prophet and seer.

Let the things that have to do with faith, hope and love stir anew within our hearts, and let our lives be guided by wisdom, gentleness and goodness, for your kingdom's sake.

Advent 4

Ever faithful God – who in the wintertime of the world sent the Christ child to harass our countryside with grace – redeem our city streets with hope, garland our weary lives with a new vision and let the light shine again in the drabness of our lives and in the dark corners of our souls.

Bestow on us the gift of contentment and freedom from regret with the hopefulness of youth, the magic miracles of childhood and that gladness of the soul which sings the songs of Zion even at midnight.

Let us be born again, anew, afresh.

Come again at this season of great hopes but also sad despairs, when homes are festooned but the homeless know there is no room in the inn, when children are delighted and children are abused, when we grow weary of the gifts that please, but give too little time for the gift that has no price.

When sadness marks our days, let hopefulness be still our companion and good dreams still crowd our nights.

For the dawn will surely come and a rocking cradle will unsettle the world with a new beginning to unseat the mighty and cause the forgotten of the earth to sing again.

For unto us a child is born and unto us a son is given; a gentle hand is placed on the shoulder of the world, and the gift of heaven shimmers in the morning light.

Surely, life will never be the same again and we give thanks.

Christmas Eve

Christmas is happening again in our strange human hearts. The century on its knees and the busy world with bowed head and needy heart. A declaration of holiness in the midst of our grasping, a story of need in the midst of our consumption, a marvel of miracle in the midst of the glitter and banal.

The weapons of warfare fall from our hands, peace calls us to its embrace and gentle greeting to those of goodwill and to all the others.

Our hearts cry out for a gladness almost forgotten yet always remembered, for a hope often forsaken yet brought alive in the cry of a little child.

Praise for the shepherd's crook, wise men hurrying and a holy mother with bowed head. Come, come, O mystery, most holy, O word shaped in love, spoken in faith and fashioned in flesh.

In the strange confusion of our time, let a star still shine to guide us in the darkness, and, in our joy, may we still catch the sound of angel voices.

For underneath the shallowness of our living, there is a longing for the beauty that does not fade, the eternal that is forever faithful and the mercy that is daily given.

Let the small, the innocent and the simple possess our souls again, and let there be the impulse of tenderness towards all, even our enemies.

We pray for those for whom the season is sad, children

lost in the folly of our times, family members in dangerous places, parents who no longer recognise family and the sadness of those who have no family to greet them and no heart to care.

Bless our families when they gather. Let great joy fill our kinship, and may the Christ child be truly born anew in our hearts. For it is a new day. This we ask, for your kingdom's sake.

Christmas Day

Ah Jesus kin, who in rude barn gathers all creation, what shall we bring this morn but sweet praise? For here is the word made flesh, here is the true light that shines in the darkness, here is the Saviour who is partisan for the poor and the forgotten.

In astonished dawn and holy morning, let angels and shepherds, let kings and common folk sing of the miracle that is come again into our poor broken world and to our poor distracted souls.

Comfort ye, comfort ye, my people with the cry for peace in a world at war, a longing for gentleness in a world of violence, a search for simplicity in a world of noise, a hope for a miracle when the old year is dying, a child trailing clouds of glory from God to touch our lives with tidings of comfort and joy.

Let joy come again to this weary and troubled world, joy to those who hunger and cry for bread, joy to those who mourn for a life that never was and a companionship that never blossomed, joy to those with ancient anger in their hearts and bitterness in their souls, joy to those who work for peace because they are at peace with themselves, joy to those who grow not weary of the search for justice because they have no truck with dishonesty.

And let peace come to our lives too, peace for the imperfection of our discipleship and mercy for every wandering, not endless striving for goodness or acceptance, but with awe and thanksgiving for the mercy that keeps no records and the love that asks no questions.

So shall we live as your sons and daughters in a good world.

New Year Opening Prayer

The psalmist says: "Our days are passed away… we spend our year as a tale that is told."

Only a night from the old to the new, only a sleep from the dusk to the dawn, only a step that the old can come true in the new, only a cry from above that light has come into the world, and grace has brought a fresh beginning to a year that had grown too old. Only the certainty that every weariness will be clothed with joy, and every step a day's march nearer home.

God of the ages, does not your love hold still our sadness and quieten the memory of that which shall be no more?

You have been our past. You are still our present. You will be our future. But as the year is new so let our lives be too.

Pardon the waste of hours, the dry seasons, the desolate evenings and the shabby dawns.

We acknowledge too high resolutions that bent too low in the face of selfish aims, too many grand declarations that were as empty as the wind, too many small goals that were still too big for smaller hearts.

In the dark of our own night, we looked into our own blind eyes.

From this time forward, dear God, let us be a new people with wide horizons, strong compassion, thoughtful faith, honest endeavour and great hope.

Set the seal of your mighty presence upon our brow and lead us forward to days that are new and unstained.

New Year Second Prayer

Most gracious God, who guided your people with a pillar of cloud by day and a pillar of fire by night, teach us to journey wisely into this pristine year – a year new, untrodden and unknown – that our days not go by desolate, drab and lost.

The future unknown yet the past not to be forgotten.

We give thanks for the light of days long gone – the parents who gave us life and then love without measure, the teachers who guided our steps and planned for our good, the family who indulged our eccentric ways and strange moods and were always there when we needed them, our fathers and mothers in faith who believed in us and prayed for us. For these, our deepest thanks.

As time must pass, we remember, too, the smiles, the tears, the victories of childhood's years – the eyes that shone, the clasp that held, the promise not broken. For these, our deepest thanks.

As time must pass, we touch again the shadows of those who were our love and life and laughter, loved and never to be forgotten, gone to ground, to dust, to sand, gone on the strong shoulders of the swift wind to a land that is fairer than day, but their star will set in the western sky.

And because the past was so rich, open the door to this new year.

"Ring out the grief that saps the mind
For those that here we see no more;

Ring out the feud of rich and poor,
Ring in redress to all mankind.
Ring in the valiant man and free,
The larger heart, the kindlier hand;
Ring out the darkness of the land,
Ring in the Christ that is to be."

Epiphany

God of the ages, since time began, men and women have sought you on mountain top and gentle brook, in wilderness where bushes have burned and in deserts where only the wind is heard, in mighty storms and a still small voice, in the confines of the mighty and in the home of a simple peasant guided by a star in the East.

In our loud and angry world, we too search like the wise men of old, for you have made our hearts restless until we rest in you and thirsty until we drink of the water of life.

In the storms of life, we will find safety under your wings. You will hold us in the darkness and we will not be lost.

Draw us in again to hear the word which shall make us whole, to the light that will overcome the darkness, to the little one who is to be cared for because his arms reach out to the whole world.

We do not bring gold, frankincense and myrrh. We bring only hearts that are loving, souls that are gentle and words that are welcoming.

We hail you, new life in the dawn of a new age, new hope for peace on earth, brightest and best of the sons of the morning.

We welcome you – heaven's gift for a world that had lost its way.

Winter Time 1

The psalmist says: "He summons up the storm clouds from the ends of the earth and brings the wind out of his storehouse."

Now are the cold days upon us. The sun has grown weak and the birds are fled, the sky is unbeginning and unending.

We march to the loneliness of the hill and the fear of the wild creatures who must find their food.

Winter strengthens our cares, and we are not wise in our own conceits.

Now are the cold days upon us.

But you, O Lord, give us a familiar world close at hand with the nearness of friends, the embrace of loved ones and an altar of faith garlanded with hope. We give our grateful thanks.

Unmaker of old ways, bringer of strange joys, beauty so ancient and yet so new, you give us good memories of the past, a Saviour's love in the present, and the Spirit leading to new truths yet to be discovered, and new paths yet to be trodden. We give our grateful thanks.

Surely, goodness and mercy do indeed follow us all our days. If strong our hearts, O God, yet sad our lives.

Too often we have set our hearts on the things that perish and starve the soul.

We are at home with injustice and at ease with the sufferings of others.

We cling to comfort more than goodness.

We are part of the sickness of our society and it finds sanctuary in our souls.

We have need of a great repentance and an even greater mercy.

Keep us steady and unafraid in the unshaped days which now lie before us. May we know that whatever comes, you come with it, and whatever befalls us, we cannot fall out of your care.

Winter Time 2

Praise God that the winter is white as well as dark, that the sun still shines after the storm is over, that birds fly blue and grey by our windows, that friends still call and loved ones remember, that children laugh and young people play.

Praise God that in the winter our eyes still look for the spring, that in the cold we have shelter and warmth, that in the nighttime fire flames dance, that our dying is in his keeping and we each arise to the day that the Lord has made.

Praise God that sin shall not have dominion over us, that our folly is never greater than his mercy, that every end is a new beginning, that his good purposes never fail and none may make us afraid.

Pardon our sins, O God, free us from the guilt of the past and prepare us for the joys of the future through Jesus Christ our Lord.

Lord Jesus Christ, in the country roads of Galilee, not all the sick found their way to your side, not all the lonely discovered the friend that sticketh closer than a brother, not all the sad at heart felt the touch of the one who wept.

They had to have their hands taken, their bodies carried, their names mentioned.

So, in our hearts, those who fear the dawn, those whose illness cannot be cured, those whose love surrounds their frail parents or their needy children but cannot heal them, those whose lives are coming to an end – shine through the gloom and point them to the skies.

Our prayers go out to lives that are now desolate and empty, the separated, the abandoned, the homeless, the despairing. O Father of us all, let none of your family be alone or forgotten. Draw them in. Lord, draw them in.

Bless all those called by the will of the people to serve the common good. Bestow on them generous integrity, compassion and perseverance, for your kingdom's sake.

Winter Time 3

Still is the winter upon us, and the night is nailed to the sky with hard bright stars. And the morning will come with cold gladness and a day of fresh tasks.

Still is the winter upon us and stands true the fidelity of a God who keeps his people in good times and bad.

Still is the winter upon us, and we know what it is to be blue and lonely, the weeping in our cities and the suffering that wounds us all.

Still is the winter upon us, and buried like seed is the springtime, the wind of the Spirit and the promise that seedtime and harvest shall not fail.

Still is the winter upon us, the voices sadly missed, the presence we have loved, bright stars well-set in the western sky.

Still is the winter upon us, yet all is well, for 'he brought me into his banqueting house and his banner over me was love'.

So, come to us, gracious God, in this holy place. Come as the truth that uproots all falsehood.

Come as the shadow of a stranger on the shore.

Come as the voice, the longing, the hope that will not be denied. Come, thou fount of every blessing.

With one voice, we speak of the deep darkness that covers our souls and leaves us lost in the night.

We are creatures of great pride and arrogant demand, the

lazy mind, the meagre trust.

We walk as blind people in a world of miracles.

We are comfortable with the shallow and the false.

We bind not your word upon our foreheads but hold fast to meanness of spirit and littleness of soul.

We are at ease with lazy discipleship and indulgent self-will. We do not easily let go of that which destroys.

O ever patient God, may we prove again that plenteous grace with thee is found, grace to cover all our sins.

Heal us, help us, restore us, for love's sake.

Winter Time 4

All things are his.

It is winter with the ring, the wrack, the cold.

The skies are wild and fleeting, the clouds are angry and the shadows adrift from the light.

All things are his.

It is winter. The singing of the birds is no longer heard in our land, the leafless trees are blind and thin and barren. They creak and groan in the cold wind.

All things are his.

It is winter. Yet, there is bread and wine on the table, the family can gather, the young are still dreaming and the old remembering.

The waiting, the hastening, the hoping are his.

All things are his.

It is winter. Yet, it is a season still for rejoicing, the happiness of a maiden, love walking towards us and hope perched in the soul.

All things are his.

It is winter. We are not alone but remembered and greatly loved.

Yet, in the winter, O Lord, sad are our hearts for the many follies of our pilgrim way, the small treacheries and shabby compromises.

Restore us. Forgive us. Draw us back to heaven – our dimly remembered home with the sound of angel voices and the cry of a child – that in the clamour of many voices we may hear your voice, and, in your absence, we may find your presence, O mystery of the ages, O mercy from on high.

Winter Time 5

O God – so mysterious and yet so near – before we first saw the moon rise in the shadows or the dawn melt the darkness, before we breathed on our own or our heart remembered, you stirred us to life and kept us safe in the gentle darkness. You formed us for knowledge, for hope, for love. You set eternity in our hearts and left us forever unprepared for your stillness – yet longing, longing to be at home.

The years of infancy have long passed, but now give us a heart to search for you, a grace to discern you and a trust to hold on to you when we must grow again through adversity, through failure and through uncertainty. And, one day, we will hear the faraway call that no other can. Then as life comes to a close – as it should – give us a quiet trust to lose the earth we know for greater knowing, to find a land more kind than home, to leave the friends we've loved for greater loving. For in life and in death, we belong to you. All shall be well, all shall be well and all manner of things shall be well.

Hear our confession and in it our sadness, regret and shame.

We are more ready to acquire than to share, more willing to demand than to give, more partial to avenge than to reconcile.

Too often we have been uncertain witnesses and faithless servants; meagre with truth, callous towards need; long on song, short on service. Pardon us. Restore us. Set our feet again on the rock that does not move and is not shaken.

Make us a symbol of hope to the weak and forgotten, to the powerless and the deceived, to the lonely and those of little account.

Make our church open to all but captive to none, save for only him – to the one who came in simple garb to redeem us at infinite cost.

It is winter and sad are our hearts and words too weak to hold up our distress that the family of humankind is still grievously broken with different colours, different persuasions, different memories. Yet, you have hidden in the soul of people everywhere a longing for peace, a place to call home, a presence to comfort, a touch to reassure, the dream of a future where all children will grow up curious with laughter in their eyes, hope on their lips and largeness in their hearts.

It is winter. Let the rain come and wash away the ancient grudge, the bitter hatred, the wound of neglect.

It is winter. Let the earth be nourished to bring forth flowers and the mountains to teach our hearts to reach up to heaven.

It is winter and the start of a new week.

Circle us, Lord. Keep protection in and danger out.

Circle us, Lord, Keep hope in and anger out.

Circle us, Lord. Keep compassion in and greed out.

Circle us, Lord. Keep fidelity in and betrayal out.

Circle us, Lord. Keep generosity in and intolerance out.

Circle us, Lord, with quiet faith, generous hope and undying love.

Winter Time 6

Here in this ancient place which has weathered ten thousand winters but welcomed ten thousand and one spring times—

Here in this sacred place which has seen the tears of loss for voices that are heard no more but also the water of deepest hope on the brow of a sleeping child and witnessed hands joined in the storm-tossed adventure of love between two searching hearts—

Here in this hallowed place where heaven touched earth, and the bush burned, and small compulsions were robed as destinies, and the soul's deep hunger fed again—

Here in this ancient, sacred, hallowed and much loved place, a serious house on windswept earth, this silence which is filled with the word of the ages—here, O God, receive our prayers – poor, faltering and imperfect though they be, as we are too.

O God, we thank you for an unforgettable man born into a peasant home, growing up in a normal noisy family, who – like us – knew laughter but also disappointment, love but also sadness – Jesus, son of Mary. Only his name is here for our healing and hope.

He sought neither wealth nor status; he confronted the proud and the powerful, the devout and the unforgiving, with the call of a shepherd for a sheep that was lost and the welcome of a father to one who had been away too long in a far country.

Our hands will be lifted up in gratitude for Jesus, a man of sorrows, God with a human face, the eternal come near. Again, our thanks for him. And, to our thanksgiving, we must add our confession and acknowledge our grievous folly.

Not just broken promises and shallow discipleship, not just untruth and betrayal, but also the forgotten wounds that have shaped our lives, the injuries we cannot forget and have not forgiven, the evil not named but accepted.

The burden of our failings is intolerable, but your mercy and forgiveness are greater still. We cling to that and we find peace.

Ash Wednesday

Most faithful God, God of the shadows, when the darkness falls and our dreams are turned to ashes, God is present still; when hope is followed by disappointment and loss, we do not ask for more power in the face of travail and discouragement but for your presence. Hold us in the losses of life when fear, doubt and loneliness are our companions. Let not the stars go out. Be still, our God, when we feel forsaken by heaven and alone on earth.

Hear now as we confess our sins in the sure confidence that a broken and contrite heart, O God, you will not despise.

We are creatures of great pride and arrogant demand with lazy mind and meagre trust.

We walk as blind people in a world of miracles.

We are comfortable with the shallow and the false.

We hold fast to anger and guilt, to meanness of spirit and littleness of soul.

We are indulgent with self-will and do not easily let go of that which destroys.

Cleanse us, O God, with hyssop and we will be clean; wash us, and we will be whiter than snow.

So shall we be at peace again and journey on in our pilgrimage.

And when our allotted years have passed and our bodies turn to dust, as is the end of all living things, when our frail hold on life turns to ashes, when we must let go of those we have known and dearly loved, hold on to us, faithful God, and give us gentle sleep in the quiet darkness until that new day shall dawn and joy flood our hearts and we greet again those we have loved long since and lost awhile. For in life and in death, we belong to you.

Lent 1

Giver of the dawn, Lord of the morning light, in this solemn season when faith must reflect in silence how trust in the Father could end in the judgement hall, let these days of pilgrimage not be stained by shallow discipleship, easy answers nor the broken promises of the soul.

In this Lenten season of stretched out days, send our roots rain so that we may grow in soul and journey on to a new day where joy and energy, courage and freedom, mercy and justice shall dare all darkness.

Let not our Lenten fast be the larder lean and clean, but a fast to dole out meat to the hungry, companionship to the forgotten, comfort to those who mourn and a home to the wanderer.

Let our Lenten fast be from old debate, from feast days where judgement does not run down as waters nor righteousness as a mighty stream, songs that have no joy and viols that have no melody.

Lord of the Lenten way, call us by name so that we may know you; call us to you so that we may live; call us into the world so that we may serve; call us to risk so that we may trust beyond ourselves.

In this Lenten season, pardon us, restore us and cause our hearts to be glad again, for love's sake.

Lent 2

It is the season of the desert and the wilderness of our uncertain journey and singing is no more. But lead us, O Lord, to a deepening life of the spirit.

Let our fast be from judgement but our feast be of warm acceptance. Let our fast be from anger but our feast be of gracious patience.

Let our fast be from discontent but our feast be of deep gratitude. Let our fast be from gossip but our feast be of gentle truth.

Let our fast be from discouragement but our feast be of rich joyfulness. Let our fast be from fear but our feast be of strong faith.

And if our thoughts and self-examination be inward, let our actions be outward and generous – bread for the hungry, companionship for the lonely, reassurance for the failures, hope for the depressed and joy again for those who have lost their way.

Teach us to be quiet and learn to wait, to be silent so that we may hear, to lay aside the goods we cherish so that we may grow in soul and thoughtfulness that we may lean more securely on that which does not change.

And if we must be sad at what we lose, with the passing of time, may we not lose ourselves in sadness but calmly accept the transience of the years so that we may be ready for eternity and weep with hope when the stone is rolled against the tomb of those we have loved long since until the new morning breaks and we will greet again those we have loved long since and lost awhile.

Lent 3

Come brooding, majestic, caring God, inform the desperate mystery of our prayers and the deep needs of our hearts.

Set in our weakness your strength, in our fear your peace, in our designs your purposes, in our losses your crown of glory that fadeth not away.

Keep our fragile lives from the snares of the Evil One, so that no bitterness, no guilt, no despair and no regrets will find an abiding place in our hearts.

Forgive our follies and the sins that have misshaped our lives, poisoned other relationships and left the world mired deeper in that which is evil.

We pray for the world in which we have not been a healing presence. Bind us together as one human family whose way is peace, whose charter is tenderness, whose motive is service and whose goal is your kingdom on earth.

Let the homeless, the lonely, the forgotten, the troubled and the despairing know victories they can count and gentleness they can trust.

Watch over every breaking heart and abide in every saddened home.

Let our good land be a hope for the little peoples of the world and a conscience for the great. Let it be a land of promise, a holy land, the home of good and generous people, for love's sake.

Lent 4

God of the refugee and God of the homeless, God of the unhappily married and God of the single parent, God of the very needy and God of the very greedy—

God of Moses who dashed for freedom and God of Korah who challenged his power—

God of Ahab who stole from a poor man and God of Jezebel who had style in her death—

God of Ezra who despised foreigners and God of Amos who loved justice—

God of John who announced the kingdom and God of Jesus who opened it to the irreligious, publicans and sinners welcome—

God of all of us gathered as one in this holy place, and God of each of us with our personal needs and private fears—

God of our past, God of our present and God who will be there whatever our future—

Receive us, hold us, keep us until the journey is over and we are safe home with those we have loved long since but never forgotten.

Chaos and confusion are on the loose as they were so long ago in the time of Caiaphas and Pilate but so is your word vested in that unforgettable man from Galilee.

Pardon us. Renew us. Restore us for our lives are haunted by grace, borne up by mercy and blessed a thousand times.

Lent 5

It is the season of the gathering darkness when hopes can be false and we wander into nowhere, but God is still near and his grace is deeper than the broken parts of our lives. It is the season of sorrow. It is the season of hope. The shadows get shorter and the green is coming to new life – Easter joy after Good Friday tears.

Set in our fevered lives, your calmness, O Lord. Set in our anxieties, your peace. Set in our sadness, your comfort. Set in our regrets, your patience. Set in our guilt, your forgiveness.

Let not self-reproach weaken the strong knowledge that we are loved as we are, not as we might be, loved and never to be forgotten, never to be a stranger to a father's welcome, never far from the lamp left burning in the window with the door ajar and the everlasting arms open to welcome and bless.

Teach us, O God, that the earth does not belong to us, but we belong to the earth.

Teach us to live with great care, endless delight, and awareness of the handiwork of the Creator.

Teach us to live with unwearied compassion and stubborn honesty. Teach us to be born again and again and again.

Make us the people of a new age and the first fruits of a new creation.

The days go slow and the years go fast.

Yet, the glad tidings are always new and of great joy. So, we give grateful thanks.

Palm Sunday

O God of the deep heavens, who places the eternal where palms are waved, children play and voices are raised in great joy; a God of the unexpected, who saddles a speechless animal, a tattered outlaw of the earth with the hopes of a waiting people, teach us to believe that for the everlasting right the silent stars are strong.

In this season, teach us to be engaged with love's austere and lonely offices. For we, too, are a people of violence, we have despoiled the holy and destroyed fidelity; a people whose discipleship is weak in performance though loud in profession; constancy absent when the Saviour goes to a cross not for our sins but because of our sins.

We humbly confess that the evil is also in us as it was in those disciples so long ago.

As today we start the solemn journey to that seething holy city of the heart, may we learn anew to set our lives in the vulnerable uncredentialled places of life that out of the fears, sadness and disloyalty we may rest wholly in you and be made ready for a God who stalks the earth with new life.

We pray for our poor world so greatly loved – loved before the church and redeemed outside a city wall.

We pray for our lost world where the hungry are not fed, the innocent not protected, the lonely not remembered and the dying not companioned.

Bless our own families, especially those far away. Their

arms are for us the arms of God. And keep in your safekeeping those we have loved who still remain in our hearts.

This we ask, for your kingdom's sake.

Good Friday

O day of deepest sadness, O hour of most cruel shame, O time of greatest loss! A day of darkness and gloom when the stars refused to shine. Now stand we with bowed heads in the shadow of the night of the starless sky, a day when a mother wept for her oldest son and the world lost its bearings.

Mary's boy child was no threat to Caesar's power but the simple call of a Galilean to purify the temple of the Most High and offer only the sacrifice of a broken heart and a contrite spirit. It was a day when brave men died for liberty and a good man died for peace.

It was the hour the prophets had foretold when the kingdom would be established with justice and righteousness. There would be no deceit in his mouth. The kingdom would come.

But God approached in tears at what we humans did to each other, for Jesus had done nothing wrong. Let the mountains fall on us and let the hills cover us for the grass is still green. Oh, let us remember and mourn awhile.

Teach us, O faithful God, now to be his true disciples, to fear no condemnation but offer a gracious acceptance in his name to all who have gone wrong, to establish a city of peace where we dwell and a land of promise where we abide. So shall all things be made new.

Lord of our darkest place, let in your light. Lord of our greatest fear, let in your peace. Lord of our deepest grudge, let in your forgiveness. Lord of our loneliest moment, let in your presence. Lord of our saddest betrayal, let in your salvation.

So shall the new age come and he who suffered be Lord of all.

Easter Day 1

O vast and gracious God, who holds us in a love that is greater than hatred and a life that is stronger than death, we give thanks for this day wreathed in gladness and belled in song.

Neither the evil 'round us or the sadness that bivouacs within our souls shall have the last word.

One stronger than death has come to our aid.

Did not the silent stars call the Easter dawn to sing?

Did not the canticles of wind and trees burst into glad praise in the garden?

Did not bread broken at eventide open eyes that were beholden?

Hearts that were burdened, lives that were bereft and regrets that were heavy knew again healing for brokenness, beloved presence for empty loss and mercy for failure.

Thus it was on that first Easter, O Lord.

Thus let it be for us again, O Lord – new beginnings, a new spirit, new life.

Let the dream sing inside us. Let the words of long ago cast a spell upon us.

Forgive our small treacheries, our shabby compromises and vacant shadows.

Pray in us the prayers of peace for a remembered past, the prayers of trust for a baffling present and the prayers of hope for an unknown future. It is a new age. Thanks be to God.

Easter Day 2

O God of the Easter dawn, who brings hope out of emptiness and new beginnings out of loss, bestow on us joy and life for the fresh tasks that lie before us as the winter now flies north.

We come praising the mystery of mercy and the certainty that death shall die.

We pray for the living – for those whose crosses are heavy, whose sorrows are deep, whose bodies are racked with pain, whose spirits are encompassed by the fiends of fear and the demons of despair, those torn from the sunlight and bound in the chains of man's hatred and cruelty, the forgotten, the disfigured, those lost in dementia, the hungry and the dying.

O God, who raised up Jesus from the dead, be faithful to all your children and give them the glad news of an Easter morning.

We pray for the dead, not bound in graveclothes but alive in Christ – names so dear, memories so treasured, presence so missed.

Let not the threads of love be broken, though they be hidden; and keep us in tryst with those who gave us life and laughter and love.

Turn us from the dead ends of our life to that which does not fade or pass away. Turn us to simple truth and a good heart, to tenderness and courage, to that path which journeys on 'gainst storm and wind and tide, that path to the city of God – our heavenly home.

For we poor mortals wear the colours of your eternity and are fashioned for glory.

Pentecost 1

O thou creative God, Spirit that moved upon the face of the waters, life stirring in the deep darkness of space, did you not come of old in fire and storm and mighty law on the mountain top?

Did you not come so that hearts might be strangely warmed again and so that the young might have their visions and the old might dream their dreams?

For unless the ear catch fire, God will not be heard; unless the eye catch fire, God will not be seen; unless the mind catch fire, God will not be known; unless the heart catch fire, God will not be loved.

Let the wind of a new age sweep through our tired ways and tepid discipleship so that we may be a new people possessed with courage, compassion, gentleness and hope.

Bless the worldwide church to which we belong and the local congregations which give us joy, life and roots. May we rightly name that which is evil and call to account those in power and wealth in the name of the poor and forgotten, and those who carry sorrows unshared.

And make us, by your spirit, a community where each shall hear in their own language the word of mercy, truth and love – for your kingdom's sake.

Pentecost 2

Sadness and loss we have known, O God, but we have never been left comfortless. In storm and cloud, in wind and fire and flame, you always come to renew, revive and cause us to sing again.

Open our hearts to receive you and our minds to recognise you.

You are the air we breathe, the distance we gaze into, the space which surrounds us. Like the wind which bloweth where it listeth, the Spirit compasses us about for care, for hope, for endeavour.

You are the kindly light in which men and women are friends with each other. You are the breath of God with which he playfully ordered the universe. You are Christ's presence with us in the sunshine and in the dark. We are not alone.

Inspire us to what is good, to faithfulness and patience, to compassion and courage, to gentleness and gratitude.

O Spirit of mercy, truth and love, we want things to be different in ourselves. Stir within us new ideas, lively thoughts, fresh visions and the ability to be the best that we can be.

We want things to be different in our church. Create a new sense of mission and purpose, a new grasp of the important issues of our time, a new appreciation of ordinary folk.

We want things to be different in our land. Let us not use

great history and great power to oppress little people, but may we be the advocates and guardians of the poor and the forgotten – in the name of him who sent us a guide and comforter, even Jesus Christ, our Lord.

Pentecost 3

O Spirit of fire and hope and holiness, Spirit that came to a dispirited and scattered people, a people of old ways and old ideas, a people without vision and without daring and you created a fire in their hearts that would never go out, we now pray for that fire to blaze again in our hearts and among our company.

Let it consume the hatred, the arrogance, the fear, the distrust by which we become enemies to one another and fragmented within ourselves. Let the joy of a new age and the hope of all who are overwhelmed discover that out of brokenness may come a new person.

Let the good dreams which live in every human heart and are unused be raised to new life.

We pray for the sad and downcast, the forgotten and the abandoned, the lonely and the lost. Watch over them as an eagle watches over her young, and let the human family in its diversity of race and religion, of generation and tongue, still be made one in spirit. May men and women everywhere be the inheritors of human dignity, peace and honour.

Let that unity in diversity possess our hearts, our homes, our churches, our nation and our world.

May the God who brooded over the chaos of the primaeval darkness and the violence of Calvary still heal our hearts through Jesus Christ, our Lord.

Summer 1

O God of the eternal, you hold the daylight in your hands and scatter the stars like diamonds against black velvet. Yet, you are Father to us, Mother round about us, voice that called us and heart that longed for us.

You are the wind of the desert, the call of the horizon, heaven come down to earth, infinite spirit born in our time, eternal whisper clothed in history. You are friend to us, name written on the palm of your hand, making us strangers no longer to each other.

You are the courage of heart to our weariness, singleness of purpose to our wandering, word of comfort to our sadness, spear of indignation to our selfishness, eternal life to our deadness.

Yet, you are judge to us, furnace of fire, difficult kinsman.

Threatened by guilt and dogged by failure, besieged by little hates and great fears, unable to love others because we do not love ourselves, weary in our sacrifice and cautious in our resolve, seeking for the truth about the world and hiding from the truth about ourselves, we can only cry 'save us, Lord; save us or we perish'.

Hold not our sins up against us but hold us up against our sins. Let the circle of your vast love capture our smallness, the fire flame out from thicket hedge, worn hands open in love, broken hearts be remade and a crust of heaven's bread be sustenance for our way.

This we ask, for love's sake.

Summer 2

In early Israel, there was no word for praying. It was simply calling, reaching, asking, trusting that the One who has no name knows my name and I will be heard. So then let us pray.

Lord God, the summer days come to us, various, wide, and the long pause of the day sets the heart dancing.

"For all things are charged with the grandeur of God. And the Holy Ghost over the bent world broods with warm breast, and with ah! bright wings."

The birds waken, the trees stir, the cities arise, the villages ring out and our hearts leap again for the dayspring from on high hath visited us.

Oh Lord, give us awe before we speak of mercy, give us wonder before we speak of grace, give us gratitude before we speak of need.

"For God – who made the earth, the air, the sky, the sea, who gave the light its birth – careth for me."

What else can we do but lift our eyes in gratitude and bow our heads in gratefulness? Bless the Lord, O my soul.

Yet, Lord, let the morning goodness deal gently with us, for we are stained in a new day which is unsullied.

Unready for opportunity, we have no expectancy; unprepared for difficulty, we have no perseverance; unused to holiness, we have no humility.

Loose us from fear and unbelief, from blindness of eyes and cowardice of spirit, from meanness of temper and idleness of hands, from judging others too quickly and ourselves too easily.

Hope still lingers with us; Lord, fulfil that hope. Love still lingers with us; Lord, channel that love.

Life still lingers with us; Lord, hold that life gently until we come to the land that is fairer than day where the angels still sing.

For love's sake.

Summer 3

O God – our dark, our silence, our mystery – whose love enfolded us before we first saw the dawn, whose touch caressed us before we were formed, whose hands kept us in the gentle darkness until the new day should arrive and whose arms will welcome us home when life's work is done, your stillness finds us ever unprepared and your mercy finds us ever in need.

We confess our grievous weakness in a world of anger and callousness, of avarice and cruelty, of an indolence that hears not the cries of the desperate and the fears of little children.

Forgive us for the world we bequeath them and the broken glory that is their new day.

We embrace bureaucracy and shun holiness.

We are comfortable with shallow words and tepid reactions.

Too little light to beat back the darkness, too little salt to change the world, too little commitment to remember the faithful and too little time to honour the quiet simple folk who seek to make this a better world.

Gracious God, let goodness again assail our hearts, compassion again inspire our wills and high ideals again capture our imaginations.

And in this brief hour when we gather together as your people, recall us to that unforgettable man who gave himself heart and soul to the world, who was more at home with the wandering and the lost than with those who thought themselves good and trusted in their own righteousness.

Recall us to that victim whose beauty was so disfigured, to that presence which we so easily miss but can never forget.

Recall us to that voice which keeps us restless until we rest in thee.

Recall us to that master who called us to love even our enemies and hold closer than a brother the weak, the lonely and those who have no one to speak for them.

Recall us to that Saviour to whom we gave our lives long ago and who still gives us life today, even Jesus Christ, our Lord.

Summer 4

O Lord, as the darkness crumbles and the night steals silently away, let the morning bring us word again of your unfailing love and the coming of the summer time be rich with the secret ripening in the fields, boys growing tall, girls delighting in beauty and the evenings green around our homes.

The days of the past week have been tall and spacious, friendships have warmed our solitary hearts, and, always, always there has been your mercy when we sought it.

How could we not start this week with thanksgiving?

Deep gratitude for families wherein we learn to love, to laugh and feel at home, for neighbours where we learn to greet and trust, for cathedral, kirk and fireside where the soul can grow, for a bent world in which compassion still arises and strangers still stop to help the confused, for a man long ago who told us of a lost son, a lost sheep, a lost coin and bade us come home – for all this and so much more, we give thanks.

Pardon what is amiss in our lives. Set us free from guilt and also from regret. Let the love we deny save us. Let the love we reject protect us. Let the love we profess strengthen us. Let the love we acknowledge redeem us, for your kingdom's sake.

Autumn 1

Now stand we on holy ground, not dimly lit sanctuary, shadowed cloister, or altar reverently fashioned by human hands but needy world redeemed, wayward world forgiven, old world made new with fresh dawn, morning chorus, dew on the hedgerow, remembrance of family, bread broken for mercy's sake and wine shared as heaven's pledge.

Dear God, over our stained lives make the sign of your peace again. This be our holy ground.

This be our holy ground that we are held in the hands of a gracious God who gathers us together as an eagle watches over her young and bears them on her wings.

This be our holy ground – a green hill outside a city wall, a cross, a tomb, a name above all other names 'for God so loved the world that he gave his only begotten son'.

For this holy world outside and for the mystery of life within, memories of victory and defeats, hopes of struggle and longing of panic and peace, world of many sounds and yet the call of the still small voice, world never fully known except by him who hears the heart and reads the wind.

For the life you have given us, for the family you have bestowed on us, for the world you have bequeathed to us, for the eternity you have set in our hearts, for the undying hope of heaven, we give thanks.

Gracious God, pardon much that is amiss in our lives. We have misused our time, squandered our talents, harboured our hostilities and feared our mortality.

In the silence of our days and the inner hunger that will not leave, may we find it proper to grow wise in this place and touch again the high and holy things, the things of ancient sanctuary, of quiet cloister and of holy altar, for your kingdom's sake.

Autumn 2

O sudden God – our dark, our silence, our beginning – whose care enfolded us before we breathed alone, whose tenderness ordained that when our eyes first saw the light of day, they were met with smiles and delight, with joy and unbounded hope. We were indeed welcomed into God's world. We were kept warm.

And in that world gifts unnumbered but none greater than life itself.

So, the time of infancy passed and we were given to the Eternal One before our hearts remembered – washed in the water and blessed in the spirit. And, in our salad days, woven into disappointment and failure were the seeds of integrity and steadfastness. Life's scars the breastplate of truth.

"Through many dangers, toils and snares, we have already come. 'Twas grace that brought us safe thus far, and grace will lead us home."

But we confess that somewhere along the way the Evil One told us that status, fame and, above all, possessions would make us richer than the song of the birds and the lilies of the field and we would be more contented than a sky filled with stars.

We fell easy prey to a false god. Our hearts grew sad. Our joy grew brittle. The evening did not bring us peace and the night conferred no rest.

But still, still the God of Abram and Isaac and Jacob, the

God of Galilee and Nazareth did not cast us off, would not let us go, loved us more than we loved ourselves and brought us safe home on his mighty shoulders as a shepherd brings home a wounded and lost sheep.

'Tis mercy all immense and free. For, O my God, it found out me. We came to you, weary and worn and sad and you let us stay.

O most gracious God, grant us now your pardon and give us a fresh start for the new week.

Let tongues of fire preserve us from the fire of our tongues.

Let gladness and gentleness accompany our steps until the night shall come again and sleep be our reward.

Autumn 3

O vast and gracious God, who straddles the night sky and lights the evening star, who watches over us in the darkness and draws back the shadows with the welcoming countenance of the morning dawn, come with simplicity to our lives this day, lives that are worn with a thousand cares.

Come with mercy to our lives for many the failings we have known. Come with patience for weak is our discipleship, uncertain our pilgrimage and fragile our faith.

Come swordsman against our easy compromises. Come as love's gamble against evil's power.

Come as laughter, come as hope and teach us joy.

Come, come, Lord, again in this ancient place and give us the things of heaven for the things of earth.

In all of us, O Lord, an ancient rage against the good, a primal loneliness far from the gentle and the holy, a sickness of the soul that will not easily let go of that which is shallow and false, a wandering that will not come home because it is at home in the far country.

O God of a great mercy and an unwearied faithfulness, forgive what we have done and what we will do again.

Restore us to wholeness, to an honest peace with ourselves and to a lively bond with others.

Guide us, O Lord, in the week which lies ahead. Should adversity come our way, give us courage; should sadness be our lot, comfort us with the mighty mercies of heaven; should failure mark our steps, raise us up and keep us true; should loss be our inheritance, teach us to hold on to that which cannot be lost and adds no sorrow.

This we ask, for your kingdom's sake.

Autumn 4

Mysterious elusive God, in our fragmented lives, we are homesick, longing for peace, for comfort, for the assurance that we are not adrift or abandoned but cared for and never to be forgotten.

Trailing clouds of glory did we come from God, who is our home. But we have lost our way.

In this season of autumnal growth, we feel the wind, blowing where it listeth, that dries our regretful tears and aching sadness; and the flame within swift and tall that with strong touch shall take this poor creature of the earth and fashion it for glory. Oh, let it be. Let it be. Spirit of mercy, truth and love, make us better people, make us new people. Let us be born again and again and again.

Oh stone of the sages, storm wind, head wind, strange wrestler at a lonely brook, you are the deep silence at our centre, our mother tongue, the shepherd's love that sought us 'o'er moor and fen, o'er crag and torrent till the night was gone'.

Do not let us go when we let go.

Weak our discipleship. Clouded our vision. Poor followers indeed. But we do not despair. For you did not come to condemn the sinner but to embarrass the righteous. And we are silent before such holiness.

You are not the God we would have chosen – mystery afar off, tenderness so near, uprooting us, surprising us, ignoring our goodness, making all things new. But you chose us and we are your people.

Our thanks for so great salvation.

Autumn 5

O Lord, joyful our hearts and glad our paths, for still is the summer upon us, and the trees are thick with green; and the noon days are canopied in sun and blue; and the gentle nights arrive in cool darkness. How could we not give thanks and bless your name?

Does not your covenant of old still stand strong and true that seedtime and harvest shall not fail? For the land sings and the pastures are clothed with flocks. How could we not give thanks and bless your name?

Despite all that would cause our hearts to fail in this angry world, we hold on to your promise that one day there will be a new heaven and new earth, and God will wipe away all tears and there will be no more death or sorrow or crying. For glory, glory dwelleth in Emmanuel's land.

O ever living God, teach us to live as your redeemed people, the first fruits of a new age, the light that is not overcome with darkness, a people of lively faith and joyful hope in a world where we have glimpsed an open tomb. Keep us close to the One who said: "Let not your heart be troubled, neither let it be afraid." Give us the grace to be the new people of tomorrow.

Hear now, O God, our confession.

We have been uncertain and faithless servants.

We have striven to acquire rather than share, to demand rather than give, to avenge rather than pardon.

We live easily with what is false and shallow.

Create in us a clean heart, O God, and renew a right spirit within us.

Take us into a new week with hopes that heal, with words that bless and with lives that are good news to those we will meet, for love's sake.

Autumn 6

Lord Jesus Christ, in the past, not all the sick found their way to your side, not all the lonely discovered the friend that sticketh closer than a brother, not all the saddened felt the touch of the One who wept.

So, in our hearts, we bring you those who fear the dawn, those whose illness cannot be cured, those whose never-failing love surrounds their parents or their children but cannot help them, those whose lives are coming to an end. Shine through the gloom and point them to the skies.

Our prayers go out to lives that are now desolate and empty, the separated, the abandoned, the homeless, the demented and confused. O Father of us all, let none of your family be alone or forgotten. Draw them in, Lord, draw them in.

Teach us that the earth does not belong to us, but we belong to the earth.

Teach us to live with great care, endless delight and gratitude for the handiwork of the Creator.

Teach us to live with unwearied compassion, stubborn honesty and unfailing joy.

Make us the people of a new age and the first fruits of a new creation. And let a virtuous populace arise to stand a wall of fire around our much-loved isle, for your kingdom's sake.

Autumn 7

O glory round about us and radiance hovering over us, presence going before us and mercy always encompassing us, now has fidelity drawn back the shades of dusk and the dawn has come to greet us. The birds waken, the trees stir, the cities arise.

May the blessing of the morning light be upon us, light without and light within; and may that light shine from our eyes on all whom we shall meet this day, and especially on those whose way is dark and whose path is hard. Make us good news to them, joy in the world and hope for the morrow.

And in this sacred place where the prayers of the generations have hallowed the walls, where the needy have found strength, the lonely companionship and the burdened forgiveness, hear us as with one voice we speak our sorrows for the darkness that leaves us lost.

We acknowledge that we are creatures of small pride and arrogant demand, the lazy mind, the meagre trust, discipleship that stays not the course and love that dies before the evening candle is done.

Deal gently with us in our follies, our wanderings and our sins, O God of great mercy.

Give us courage to embrace forgiveness. Give us courage to forgive ourselves. And make us a new people for a new week.

Autumn 8

As across the good earth summer's golden colours gladden the heart and delight the eyes, so now we lift our hearts in gratitude for a world charged with the kindliness of God.

We give thanks for the sunlight which runs along our path.

We give thanks for the comfort of our homes and the friendships which enrich our days.

We give thanks for tasks to do and the evening to grow wise in. We give thanks for bread and wine for the journey, and for the memories which bring no sorrow.

We give thanks for this one short hour when our little lives are touched with heaven's majesty.

We will indeed bless the Lord and forget not all his benefits.

Hear also our confession, O God of a great mercy.

Forgive our tepid discipleship, our quiet dishonesties, our lazy compassion and our failure to identify that which is truly evil in our day. Mercy, mercy still to aid us. Peace, peace still to come to us.

Teach us that we are not made righteous by being right, that we are not justified by greater striving, that we are not made whole by laying up treasures on earth, that we do not find contentment by excelling others. For the lilies of the field toil not, neither do they spin, and yet Solomon in all his glory was not arrayed like one of these.

Lord, centre our lives down this day on the things that

feed the soul and enrich without loss.

Establish us strong as a virtuous people to whose ancient grandeur the stranger will always be welcomed, the poor always be cared for, the lonely always companioned and the dying always held close, for love's sake.

Autumn 9

O mighty God, who orders the seasons and bids the darkness flee before the morning light, who gathers up the dew in the arms of the dawn and makes glad our hearts in the noonday sun, stand us now on holy ground, deepen us in a growing and questioning faith green as a leaf and prepare us for fresh adventure.

Let not our anxious busyness drown out the singing of creation, or the pursuit of goods blind us to the colours and splendours of your world.

Dear God, frail our lives and uncertain our course.

When fear and confusion approach, when regrets are strong and will not retreat, when guilt and self-disappointment weigh down our spirits, when contentment has fled and the night hours bring no rest, hold on to us, hold on to us, gentle Lord, and let what is broken be healed and what is unforgiveable be met with a mightier grace.

For we belong to you, in our beginning and in our ending. Neither height nor depth, neither that which is past nor that which is to come, shall separate us from the love which from our birth over and around us lies. It is enough.

Pardon our sins. Remake our lives. Gladden our hearts, for love's sake.

Autumn 10

O eternal God, source of our being and goal of our living, Invisible – we glimpse you; unknowable – we call you by name; afar off – we feel you near like the brush of a linnet's wings, like a gentle dew upon the place beneath, like the wind that brings seed to the fertile ground and life to our bodies, and the dream of being born anew.

In you, all things consist. The very atom is light energy, the grass is vibrant, the rocks move. Touch but a stone and an angel smiles.

In your many splendored world, etched with glory, what need have we for temples made with hands save for as a place to meet friends in Christ, a place to be abased before so great a mystery, a place to lift up our hands in thanksgiving and to be welcomed home by a great grace?

We thank you for the Creator's world, blazoned in majestic mountains and hidden in a million crevices.

You came calling our name and would not be silent until we were found.

Pardon much that is amiss in our lives.

We have lied to ourselves about ourselves, resisting the truth, so in love with the dark.

We have been unfaithful to the courage and goodness in others, unresponsive to the hopes and fears of those who meet us on our path.

Forgive us now, we pray, and send us forth to strive with

all that is tawdry, all that is greedy and mean, all that is small in a world so wondrously made. This we ask, for your kingdom's sake.

Autumn 11

Lord God, who scatters the stars and holds the daylight in lively hope, work in us the miracle of grace for today, mercy for yesterday and trust for tomorrow.

You alone know the human heart, the depths of its loneliness, the breadth of its emptiness, the width of its sadness. We are bruised in the business of living and wounded in the long journey from earth to heaven.

Lord of our darkest place, let in your light. Lord of our greatest fear, let in your peace.

Lord of our longest grudge, let in your forgiveness. Lord of our deepest anger, let in your gentleness.

Lord of our loneliest moment, let in your presence. Lord of our worst self, let in your wholeness.

To our petitions this day we now add our thanksgiving.

Gratitude for the vision splendid of hills adorned in sunlight and glens clothed in crimson and gold.

Thanks for the gentle watchfulness of the moon and the wondrous glory of the everlasting stars.

Thanks for each new day loosed from the night's darkness and unstained by folly.

Thanks for a mother's care, a father's blessing, a child's trust, a companion's devotion, a friend's embrace.

Thanks for the moments of stillness and places sacred for the soul where we are no longer adrift but anchored in the past, no longer strangers in a strange land but pilgrims in a great company of the redeemed.

Thanks for the good land in which we dwell with shared diversity – a new people in an old land.

Forgive us for being casual with the truth and self-absorbed, preferring safety over the breakers and security over the storm, failing to believe that our plans can be broken but not our lives, for we have an anchor that keeps the soul steadfast and sure when the billows roll.

Bring hope out of emptiness and new opportunities out of loss, for love's sake.

Autumn 12

O God, from whose presence we flee and whose judgement we fear, and yet without whose tender care and gracious love we cannot live and dare not die, you long for us in your holiness and we long for you in our frailty.

Let the simple eucharist of ordinary things – a gracious greeting, a warm smile, an unexpected gift – be for us this day avenues of grace and personal renewal.

We long for the peace that casts no shadow, for the contentment that harbours no uncertainty and for the gentleness that is as a sunflower – safe and secure – at home in the sunlight as the circling planets hum with total joy. In this world of fear and uncertainty, of sadness and regret, we are homesick for heaven.

Pardon our sins – both great and small – so that guilt may not burden us.

Enter our darkness and surprise us with joy. Touch our minds to know you, our hearts to love you, our wills to serve you and our lives to embrace you.

When grief comes, hold us close. When failure descends, be closer than a brother and dearer than a sister. When the final darkness begins to fall, quieten our fears and take us home, for love's sake.

Autumn 13
The Day WW2 Started

Thou sudden, unexpected God, brooding in the night in its mystery, dawning the day in its newness, now are our eyes filled with glad hope for whatever comes in the untraced hours that lie before us; you come with it and we run to meet mercy and grace, gladness and joy in the clasp of family, the love of friends, the pardon of a Saviour.

We thank you this day for a life so rich in blessings, so little deserved, too lightly accepted, too seldom savoured.

Though our eyes shone with light like the sun, though our feet were swift as hinds, though our mouths were filled with song, yet they could not encompass the bounty of your gifts so richly bestowed on us.

Yet, all is not well with us. We fumble our way through life as the ancients wandered through the wilderness in search of a land of promise, sometimes feeling lost but never totally so, for a rainbow reminded the ancients after the storm was over about the faithfulness of a God who does not desert. And we too are always shadowed by human care and love divine. Goodness and mercy have indeed followed us all our lives.

And to our thanksgiving, we now add our intercession. For with one voice, O God of all people, we speak our sorrows for the sadness that comes to those whose families are broken and loved ones lost in the anger and hatred that mark the human condition. Watch over every breaking heart, bind up every troubled spirit, abide in every grieving home that joy may come in the morning.

And we recall again that time so long ago when the lights went out all over our much-loved isle and no one could stop it; chaos came with monstrous cruelty and a dark cruelty that knew no bounds; a terrible violence slew the innocent and the children of the innocent; a monstrous evil had to be stopped.

We are grateful that our angry world was not cast away in its sin but held still in the arms of a God whose love never grew weary. Foes became friends and dear ones were not forgotten. Hear this our prayer, for love's sake.

Autumn 14

Gentle God, fill this weekend with new truths not yet grasped, new insights not yet seen, new places not yet visited and new vows not yet honoured. Let wholesome things that are true and lovely crowd our leisure time so that our fretful lives may yet again learn to be at peace.

Holy God whose name is not honoured by our songs, nor our devotion by our prayers if the hungry are not fed, and the stranger not welcomed within our gates, hear us as we pray for the lands that gave us birth; make strong the voices that cry out for justice and fairness.

Draw near to the lives that have no music, to hearts that are lonely and forgotten, to souls that have lost courage and hope. Let each dawn be a bright new beginning.

We offer our prayers for those who will die too young and the road not travelled. We also offer our prayers for those whose friends have long since gone, those for whom kirk and fireside, laughter and greeting place have something of their friendliness resigned.

Bless our parents in loving memory or gracious embrace, who sat beside us when nightmares abounded and sleep was far away. They never ceased to want the best for us.

Bless our children, our delight and undimmed hope for the future; may they live well despite the untidy world we give them.

So shall all generations bless your name while young and old lie down together as the journey ends.

Hear this our prayer, for love's sake.

Autumn 15
Battle of Britain Sunday

Lord God, we give thanks for this good land, a land blessed with health, peace and sweet content.

We give thanks for the clamorous seasons which come and go.

And, especially on this day, with remembrance of times past, we give thanks for that rugged breed of men and women who stood a wall of fire around this much-loved isle.

Friendless and fearful, they were not alone.

You raised them up to soar o'er mighty mountains; you raised them up to walk on stormy seas; you raised them up to go swift-winged through the skies; you raised them up so that we, their children's children, might bless their name and tell again the mighty deeds of yore.

Keep strong in our hearts a true gratitude and deep silence for those who gave their all to keep us free.

Keep alive in our hearts what great sacrifice was called for to lay the proud invader low and cast from the earth a monstrous evil.

Yet, it was not just the might of our hand. For without the Lord, would not the waters have overwhelmed us and the flood gone over our soul? Was not the God of Abram and Isaac and Jacob our fortress and our high tower? We bless that mighty name and now give thanks.

May we honour the memory of the brave by being the

hope of small peoples, the strong companion of the weak, a haven for the poor, the homeless, the tempest-tossed, those longing to be free.

Let not ease cloud our souls in these later days nor avarice possess our lives. Let us not grow blind to that which is casually evil in our time.

Keep us alert, mindful that honour and kindliness, truth and compassion, must be protected, for your kingdom's sake.

Autumn 16
Harvest

Lord of the ripening season that now runs to meet us, when the gold is deepening down and the fruits are in their russet mantle clad, and the green is rich and ready, and the promise of old stands strong again that seedtime and harvest shall not fail, how could we not give thanks?

Lord, now is the joy come again upon us, hope brims in the crisp air and blessings unnumbered remind us of what the Lord has done. So we give thanks.

The colours of your rich creation are everywhere and the clamorous sounds of the land gladden the heart, so we give thanks.

Never has your care failed. Never has your goodness fled. Never has your bounty deserted. Never has your love grown weary. So we give thanks.

The very stones would cry out and the rocks weep if our voices were not raised in gratitude.

Guilt and sadness, wrong doing and iniquity, sorrow and tears must wait. For the good hand of the Lord is mightily upon us and gladness is in our hearts.

And yet, Lord, as we give thanks, we ask for new grace.

Deliver us from the littleness of spirit and the meanness of heart that grasps rather than gives, that keeps rather than shares, that is ungenerous to those who have no homes, unmoved by those who have no families, untouched by those who have little goods but great needs.

Set our minds against the godlessness of greed, the smallness of high walls and closed gates. "For the love of God is broader than the measure of our minds, and the heart of the eternal is most wonderfully kind."

All is not well with us.

We have wasted our substance; we have been profligate with time; we have feared our mortality.

Strangers to death, we are not at home with life. We have embraced the shadows. We have clung passionately to half-truths.

Forgive us and show us how to be the people we are called to be – redeemed, free and glad in Jesus Christ.

Autumn 17

Most gentle God – in this place of faith and doubt, this place of hope and longing, this place which knows the hunger in our souls – hear us as we reach out in prayer for others.

Bless those who rule over us. Let them not grow weary in well doing, or forget the forgotten, or count as naught the weak and the poor, for of such is the kingdom.

Bless the country we love the best but also all the lands which gave us birth. Came we not there, the little child, to the waters and the wild, to the hands that lifted us up and the voice that reassured us and the Saviour that redeemed us?

Bless our enemies. May those who have done us grave wrong still find your mercy as we have.

As a shepherd gathers the lambs in his arms and a mother tends her young, surround with a great tenderness those whose lives are sad and grievously wounded, your namesakes darkened in our midst, an old man in a park, a young mother on her own, a child unwanted, a life beset by fears, a heart made lonely by the passing of the years, a home where laughter and love have fled.

Be thou their strong tower, and let not the fires harm them nor the waters overflow them.

O faithful God, hold on to our broken and angry world – a world so greatly loved – until the dawn shall come again, and the earth be filled with the glory of the Lord as the waters cover the sea.

O caring God, receive our prayers tenderly, our dreams gently and our sins mercifully, and may those we have remembered today in this holy place prove again the ancient promise that goodness and mercy have followed us all the days of our life.

Autumn 18

O God – whose stillness is more terrible than earthquake, wind and fire – the morning light is yours, dipping into noontide; the spring is yours, dipping into summer; languid time is yours, dipping into measureless eternity.

And the present is ours with mountains to be climbed, valleys to be explored, friendships to be savoured and evenings to grow wise in. And, always, always love to surround us, grace to protect us and the light left on to welcome us home.

O God, we thank you on this most amazing day for those who gave us life – the women who touched our lives and watched over us, who comforted us in our nightmares and were a healing presence when sleep was far away. Their stars are well-set in the western skies.

And the men who fashioned our dreams and protected childhoods' steps, who taught us to trust ourselves to the winds and be confident in the tides. In their strength, were they not tender, and in their tenderness, were they not strong? We give you thanks.

But, most of all, we give you thanks for the one who came not just to give us life but life abundant and opened unto us the gates of heaven. A simple child in a lively family, in a peasant village who healed the sick, calmed the distressed and welcomed the non-religious.

Enable us to walk in his ways, to abide in his word and to

trust in his mercy.

Hear us as we pray for his darkened namesakes in our midst – the lonely, the forgotten, the poor, the bewildered and the lost. Bless and keep them in your love as you do us.

Autumn 19

O God – from whom we flee but whose presence will not desert us and whose love will never abandon us, whose stillness is more terrible than earthquake, wind or fire – speak to our emptiness, invade our loneliness and dawn upon our blindness; heal what is broken in our world. Strong hope flung against despair, justice to right what is wrong, peace to overcome conflict.

Like the seer of old, we would be watchmen for a new heaven but even more for a new earth. For this earth, we know, is soaked in blood, tears and sweat. It is disfigured with hunger, greed and misery. It is shamed with camps for those with no place to call home and no voice to say 'welcome, you were missed'.

Lord God, how can we be such a broken family in a world where love shone forth as the dawn's first light, and hope was heard in the cry of a peasant child, and forgiveness came in the tones of a Galilean outside a city wall? How can this be?

Leave, ah, leave us not alone – though our heart condemn us, though sorrows like sea billows roll – for all our hope on thee is founded.

Hear our prayers for this needy world.

Watch over every breaking heart and abide in every saddened home. Give to the forgotten, the troubled, the dying the peace they need and the companionship that does not grow weary or leave.

We pray for those who find no joy in their work and no honour in their labours.

We pray for those who cannot find work and whose work is dangerous.

We pray for single parents, alone and overwhelmed with the demands of life.

We pray for those whose loved ones are losing touch with the memories that bind and the families they once knew.

Oh God of a great compassion, do not leave us in the dark places of our lives, nor abandon us to the changes that separate us from those who need care and love. Let your kingdom come, come quickly, on earth as it is in heaven, for love's sake.

Autumn 20

God of the poor, friend of the weak, comfort of the sad, lover of the forgotten, healer of the sick, who, in a country preacher with a Galilean brogue came not to condemn the ungodly but to unsettle the righteous, make us one with all those who cry for justice and struggle for truth, who are the unwearied voice of those who have no voice, and the faithful support of those who daily refuse what is evil.

Lord God, we are no perfect community but stained a thousand times; no holy church but a stumbling guide.

And yet we call out your name, and remember in this place where the walls are stained with the prayers of the saints, the moments when heaven touched earth, the clouds parted and the angels of God ascended and descended.

We reach out to touch your dusty garment and you let us stay. I came to Jesus as I was weary and worn and sad and found in him my resting place and he has made me glad.

Hear us as we pray for all children, those who are small and defenceless, that they may not miss the magic of childhood or lie down at night with fear. Let not the world's anger hurt them or teach them to hate.

Hear us as we pray for our young people. May they not cling to the false gods of greed and intolerance but gladly enter into the service of that which is noble and true.

Hear us as we pray for the elderly that with diminished strength of body and mind, they may still have their visions and dream their dreams. May they not be subject to fear or loneliness, nor be lost in the evening shadows of life.

Hear us as we pray for those who are forgotten and not loved by anyone in particular. We remember women who are deserted and those whose minds are filled with the terrors of the imagination.

We pray for all whose days are dark and lonely. Take good care of them and bring them through the night to a new day, for love's sake.

Autumn 21

Strange and unexpected God – furnace of silence, difficult friend, so elusive, so inescapable – we judge the poor, you embrace them; we judge the angry, you love them; we judge the failed, you crown them; we judge the powerful, you care for them.

Mend our world, so grievously broken; heal our lives, so deeply compromised.

Wrap the mantle of a father's care around those whose courage is broken and whose hope is gone.

Wrap the tenderness of a mother's love around those whose grief is unhorizoned and whose fears are unquenchable.

Go on loving your world to distraction. Go on loving. Leave us not alone. Still support and comfort us.

Mysterious God – voice in the gloaming, call at eventide, shadow across a rock, stranger at a brook, murmur at a cave, cry on a hillside – let gladness dwell in our island nation. We give thanks for the variety of its folk and the diversity of its tongue. Let glad hope and warm hospitality adorn the lintel of our homes. May they be places of laughter and love, security and service, resting and rising, eating and drinking in your name.

Keep under the care of your protecting wings loved ones far away. Be faithful friend to those who lose their way, tender guide to those who get confused and watch over us as you watched over an old man in an ark and a young man on a cross.

Give us this day blue skies for our hopes.

Give us this day power to bend but not be broken by the storms of life. Give us this day sunlight to run along our path.

Give us this day memories that bring no sorrow.

Give us this day a short hour to leave our little lives with a touch of heaven's majesty, for your kingdom's sake.

Autumn 22

Trusting the day will merge into eventide with mercy; trusting the snowdrifts will transform into meadows; trusting the wild geese will return, the swallow will sing her song, and seedtime and harvest will not fail; trusting that the deer will survive the winter and the strong mountains guard the gentle valleys; trusting that he will come as a swordsman against the lies we trade and the death we choose.

O welcoming God, in the coming season of contemplation and expectation, let joyous thoughts and holy dreams prepare us for life's true quest.

Interrupt our comfortable lives with your presence, touch our possessiveness with your poverty, surprise our guilt with your healing touch and give us courage to do what is right.

Let the closing year be crowned with wisdom, with joy and true content.

Let the ravelled web we weave bring us home to heaven's gate.

O God of the nations, bless our dear native soil – the land we love the most. Deliver us from greed and arrogance, from worldly goals and pompous pleasures. Let virtuous toil and friendly companionship mark our common ways.

Our times are in thy hands. The future is alive with opportunity, gladness and advancing grace. And all is well. All is well.

Autumn 23

Stir up your power, O God; and as the year comes to the time of the gathering dark and the creeping cold, the winter storm not far away and the giant trees are naked before the cold wind, let it also carry the memory of an ancient promise and a shadow over a Jewish girl. It is the season of sadness. It is the season of hope.

When snowflakes fall, let heaven's mercy garland them; when the fire blazes in the winter gloom and the evening candles are lit, let our dreams be of a star in the sky, a light to banish the darkness and far off songs of comfort and joy. It is the season of hope.

Many the sadness we have known and many the stumble has been our lot. And, yet, yet goodness and mercy have indeed followed us all the days of our life, and we believe that this broken world will one day fall on its knees, and peace come to this poor earth, peace to those of goodwill and also to all the others. It is the season of hope.

Hear us, gentle God, as we pray for your namesakes, darkened in our midst, those who weep as the year begins to die, those who grieve for the future of children they cannot protect or clothe or feed, those whose voice is not heard and cries not answered, those who face days without friends or family. It is the season of hope.

O Father of us all, let none of your family be alone or forgotten. Draw them in, Lord, draw them in. It is the season of hope.

Strengthen and bless those whose only weapon against the power of the strong and the cruelty of the ruthless is the care they go on providing for the families who flee and the children who cry, that stubborn compassion that will not surrender to the cold shingles of a lost world. Their arms are the arms of God. It is season of hope.

Funeral Prayer 1

God of the dawn and God of the sunset, God of the first light and God of the evening star, God from whose breath we came and to whose tender care we will one day return, now has our life grown sadder and our joy become thinner, for we must sweep up the heart and put away those glad words of greeting which we shall use again until heaven's morning breaks and earth's vain shadows flee.

Yet, though our hearts are sad and our song quieter, the morning light still crowds the mountain rim, laughter is not gone from children's *eyes*, joy is not lost in the winter skies and those whom _____ loved so well will hold our hearts when they are sad.

Without him, lonelier our way. Yet for him the glory of a new day. Life not taken away but life forever changed.

O age, farewell! O weakness, farewell! O mortality, farewell!

So, let the wind die down and the storm clouds pass. Let the evening come. A soul gay and glad in new array now leaves.

For him, no darkness for a man has Christ and is not he the light of the world?

For him, no twilight for a man has Christ and is not he the bright and morning star?

For him, no loss for a man has Christ and is not he the resurrection and the life?

"Let not your heart be troubled." But it is. It is.

My friend is gone. O Comforter, where is now your comforting?

But this I know that the angels of heaven led him to that land where there is neither darkness nor dazzling, and the first words he heard were 'welcome home'.

My friend is gone. O Comforter, where is now your comforting?

And yet I treasure in my memory his gift of charity, his dear heart's ease and the honour of his amity. For these once mine, my life is rich with these. And I scarce know which part may greater be: what I keep of him or what he takes from me.

My friend is gone. But friendship has no considered end. "Nothing ill come near thee. And renowned be thy grave."

Dear God, draw near to the family whose best treasure is no more. May they know that while weeping may endure for a season, they will be whole again and cease upon the midnight with no pain.

Let that name be spoken with great joy in the home where _____ was laughter and love, the name of someone not far away but near, not forgotten but greatly cherished. For the setting impairs not the orb. The sunset diminishes not the dawn.

Into your hands, we commit _____. Into your hands, we commit his family. Into your hands, we commit ourselves. And in Jesus' name, we are strong to say amen, amen.

Funeral Prayer 2

Gracious and caring God, we are gathered here to give thanks for _____ for all that she meant to us and to that circle of friends which far extends beyond our present company.

Shaken in happiness yet sure in faith, saddened in spirit yet steadfast in hope, with the poverty of presence but the treasure of the years, how could we not give thanks for her life?

Let the evening come. Let the shadows fall. Her star is well-set. She is at peace. All is well.

How good you were to give us _____ for a lifetime. It was too short, but there was no meeting without gladness, no parting without blessing.

For us, it was a privilege and we thank you from the depths of our heart.

Her smile made the way seem gentler, her touch made the hour seem friendlier, her clasp made the world seem safer, her words made the path seem wiser.

Let the evening come. Let the shadows fall. Her star is well-set. She is at peace. All is well.

We give thanks for her many gifts, for the love and laughter she shared, for her courage in abundance and always her generosity and warmth.

Let the evening come. Let the shadows fall. Her star is well-set. She is at peace. All is well.

So, dear God, prepare us too for our own departing. For

one day, the curtain must fall and the play be done and out will go that poor light which is the last of us, like a leaf that falls and is no more, like water scattered on the ground that cannot be gathered up. The family on earth smaller so that the family in heaven might be more complete.

    And as we must soon part and go our separate ways, let the evening come. Let the shadows fall. _____'s star is well-set. She is at peace. And all is well. All is well.

Prayer on the Death of a Child

Dear God, our hearts are heavy with sorrow too deep for words and grief that has no horizon. Comfort what is beyond comfort and let gratitude bind up what is so grievously broken.

We hallow these sacred moments with thanks for what this little one meant to us. We give thanks for the gift of life to him/her in the first place. We are so grateful that his/her experiences were of love, care and tenderness, that life did not have the harshness and fear that are part of our common lot. And if the important thing in life is not its duration but its purity, then this little life – too short – was perfect in the only way that really matters. It is well with the child. Yes, it is well.

O gentle God, keep our frail craft when the river runs too swift, the current is in tumult and sleep is far away.

Calm our sadness with the knowledge that one day the light will shine again, the glad morning will dawn and we will be home, safe home at last with innocence embraced and never to be let go again and the family complete.

Hear the prayer in our sorrows and grant us peace in the gentle memories that will never fade, for love's sake.

Baptismal Prayer 1

Most gracious God, we are grateful for family life.

Here all deep and worthwhile experiences are found from birth's salutation to death's last goodbye, because here we learn that we belong, here we learn to trust, here we learn to receive that love which is the very source of our lives.

Richly bless this family. Send this child well-loved into a world in need of much love. Give to the parents the patience, wisdom and hope that they will need in the years ahead.

Help us to spoil this child with encouragement, kindliness, reassurance and, above all, with joyful expectation.

May we never belittle his accomplishments, dampen his enthusiasm, deny his vision, devalue his hopes or mute his song.

We rejoice that he is the visible sign of your covenant with us and your unfailing faithfulness to our generation.

And when our vigour wanes and our vision is dimmed, as time will decree, may he carry forward service to the needy and love for the forgotten with all the potential that now lies, waiting to be awakened in him, for your kingdom's sake.

Baptismal Prayer 2

Gracious God, let the spirit of grace and goodness attend this little girl from this day forward.

Let her have happy songs at play and gentle songs at night.

Let her be peaceful in sleep and joyful in waking, feel at home in the world and at home in herself.

When she opens her eyes, may the first thing she sees be a smiling countenance, a red cardinal, trees decked in crimson and gold, things of beauty which are a joy forever.

When she opens her ears, may she hear music and laughter, the words of precious belonging and a gentle name.

When she opens her hands, may she feel another hand outstretched in strong kindliness.

When she opens her heart, may she find love and security, and everything that will make the fragile self feel alive and contented. When she opens her soul, may she know all regrets banished and all weaknesses made perfect in the love of a Saviour.

And when the needs of infancy finally give way to the vulnerabilities of age, let her not feel alone or be forgotten but loved, remembered and deeply cherished.

This we ask in the name of all our children and in the name of the friend of children, even Jesus our Lord.

Wedding 1

Lord of our lives, let a rich blessing rest on X and Y in the promises that they have here made to each other. Grant that the courtesies, thoughtfulness and self-giving, which have laid the foundation of their love build the home that is raised on it.

As their destinies shall be woven of one pattern, their perils and joys not be known apart, so may your presence renew their affection and protect their steps. May they always return to each other in warm and generous acceptance.

Teach them to be sensitive to each other's needs, to be wise and loving parents, to be loyal and joyful friends. Reveal to them the joy of being man and wife with new places to visit, new sights to see, new friends to make and a new life to build together. May they discover the power of love not only to delight but also to heal and help, to wipe away the tears and learn to start afresh.

Let respect be the garland of their love, fidelity the companion of their ways and room to grow the hallmark of their commitment. May each appoint the other guardian of his solitude.

And in a world where there is much bitterness and sadness, anger and resentment, make them the living symbol of that love which does not wane but is fresh for each new day.

Bless their home and make it a haven of peace and a joy to all who enter it. This we ask, for love's sake.

Wedding 2

O God, who – before time began – knew it was not good for man to be alone, bless this couple as they entrust life's happiness to each other. Delight them with the lovely seasons of the body, the awakening of each other's dreams, the awe before mysteries given and received.

Sing in their home the music of hospitality. Give them patience in times of confusion, gentleness in times of conflict and generosity in times of failure.

May they learn how to sense each other's feelings, how to bear each other's burdens, how to lighten each other's sorrows and how to trust each other in times of distance. So may they face life together, whatever it may bring, with courage and great gladness.

Bless the two families brought closer today through this glad event. May they always support and enrich this new relationship.

So may we prove that the enrichment of each of us is the enrichment of all of us, and the love of all of us is the benediction that rests on the head of each.

This we ask, for love's sake.